AF588489

GREEK MYTHOLOGY

HADES

BY HEATHER C. HUDAK

CONTENT CONSULTANT
ALISON C. TRAWEEK, PHD
ADJUNCT INSTRUCTOR OF GREEK AND ROMAN CLASSICS
TEMPLE UNIVERSITY

Kids Core
An Imprint of Abdo Publishing
abdobooks.com

abdobooks.com

Published by Abdo Publishing, a division of ABDO, PO Box 398166, Minneapolis, Minnesota 55439.

Printed in the United States of America, North Mankato, Minnesota.
102021
012022

Cover Photo: Shutterstock Images
Interior Photos: Shutterstock Images, 4–5, 12–13, 14 (gods), 17, 22, 26, 28 (top), 28 (bottom); North Wind Picture Archives/AP Images, 6; Picturenow/Universal Images Group/Getty Images, 9; iStockphoto, 10, 14 (mountains and sea), 18, 29 (top); Nikola Tanchevski/Shutterstock Images, 14 (underworld); Juergen Ritterbach/Alamy, 20–21; Chronicle/Alamy, 24; Alida Latham/Danita Delimont/Alamy, 25, 29 (bottom)

Editor: Alyssa Sorenson
Series Designer: Ryan Gale

Library of Congress Control Number: 2021941515

Publisher's Cataloging-in-Publication Data

Names: Hudak, Heather C., author.
Title: Hades / by Heather C. Hudak
Description: Minneapolis, Minnesota : Abdo Publishing, 2022 | Series: Greek mythology | Includes online resources and index.
Identifiers: ISBN 9781532196775 (lib. bdg.) | ISBN 9781098218584 (ebook)
Subjects: LCSH: Hades (Greek deity)--Juvenile literature. | Mythology, Greek--Juvenile literature. | Gods, Greek--Juvenile literature.
Classification: DDC 292--dc23

CONTENTS

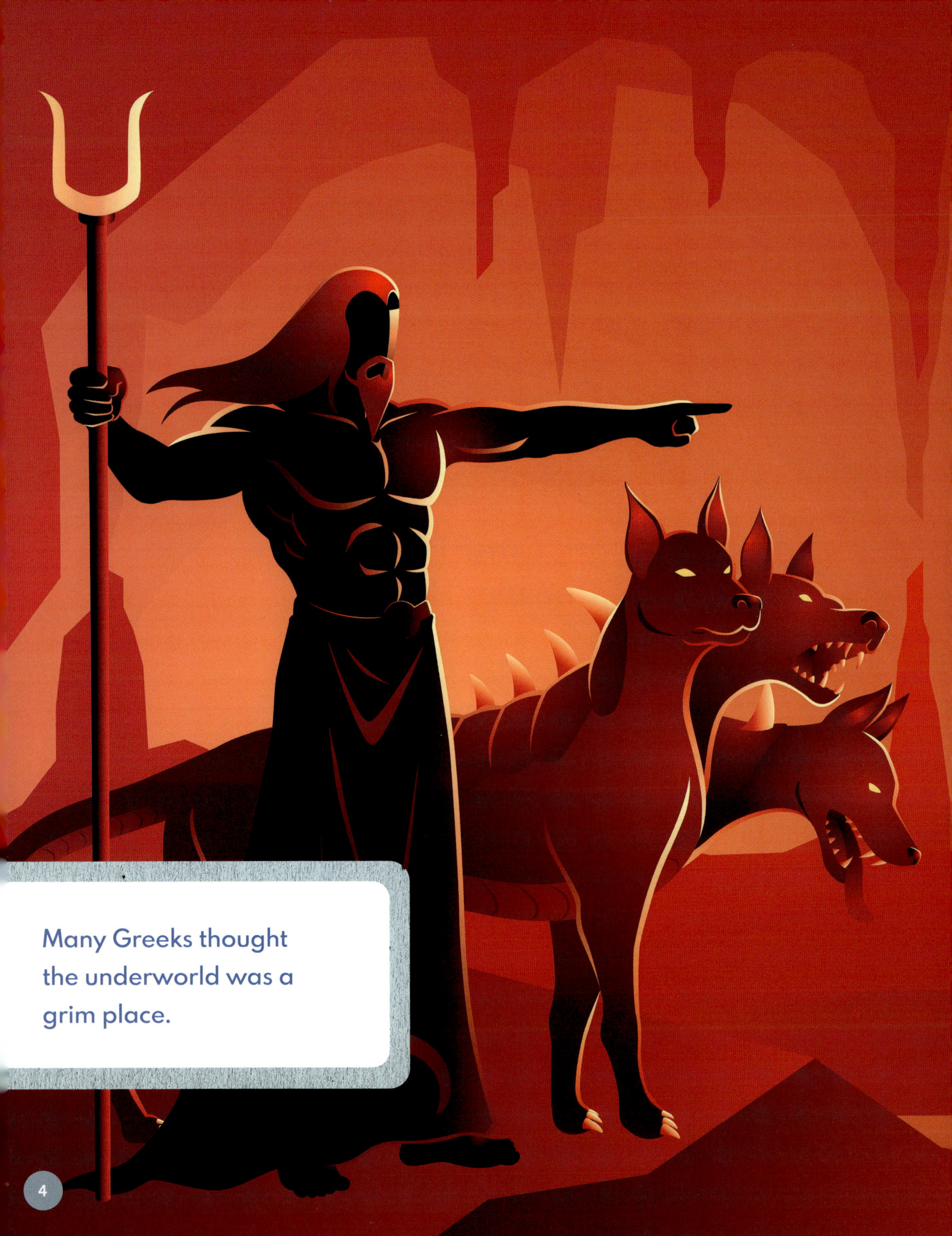

Many Greeks thought the underworld was a grim place.

CHAPTER 1

GOD OF THE UNDERWORLD

Hades was the god of the underworld. That was where human **souls** went after death. Hades was lonely and wanted a wife. He decided to bring the goddess Persephone to the underworld. One day, Persephone was picking flowers.

Some myths say Zeus encouraged Hades to quickly grab Persephone if he wanted to marry her.

The ground cracked open. Hades appeared in front of her. He grabbed Persephone. Hades rode off with her in his golden **chariot** pulled by black horses.

Demeter was Persephone's mother. She was the goddess of crops. Demeter was upset that her daughter had gone away. The crops on Earth started to die. People began to starve.

Zeus was the king of the gods. He asked Hades to bring Persephone back. But she could return only if she hadn't eaten any food in the underworld. She would be bound to Hades if she had.

The Underworld

Ancient Greeks believed that the underworld was hidden from the living. It was a dark place with no daylight. Some people called it the land of the dead. People also simply named it Hades.

Hades agreed to let Persephone go. But first he tricked her into eating a seed. Zeus had to make a choice. He could either let the humans starve or come up with another plan. Zeus decided Persephone had to spend part of each year with Hades.

Demeter was sad when Persephone was gone. This caused winter. Spring started when Persephone came home. Demeter was so happy that flowers bloomed and crops grew. The ancient Greeks believed this was why the seasons changed each year.

Greek Mythology

The ancient Greek **civilization** existed more than 2,000 years ago in southeastern Europe.

Demeter, *left*, was overjoyed when Persephone came home.

Today, thriving Greek cities surround ancient ruins.

The ancient Greeks were known for their work in math, art, science, and writing. They often told stories to explain the ways of the world. Many of these stories featured gods, goddesses, heroes, and monsters. These stories are known as Greek mythology.

The ancient Greeks believed each god and goddess had different powers. People thought the gods would help and protect them. They also believed the gods could punish them. Hades was one of the most powerful gods in Greek mythology.

Further Evidence

Look at the website below. Does it give any new evidence to support Chapter One?

Hades

abdocorelibrary.com/hades

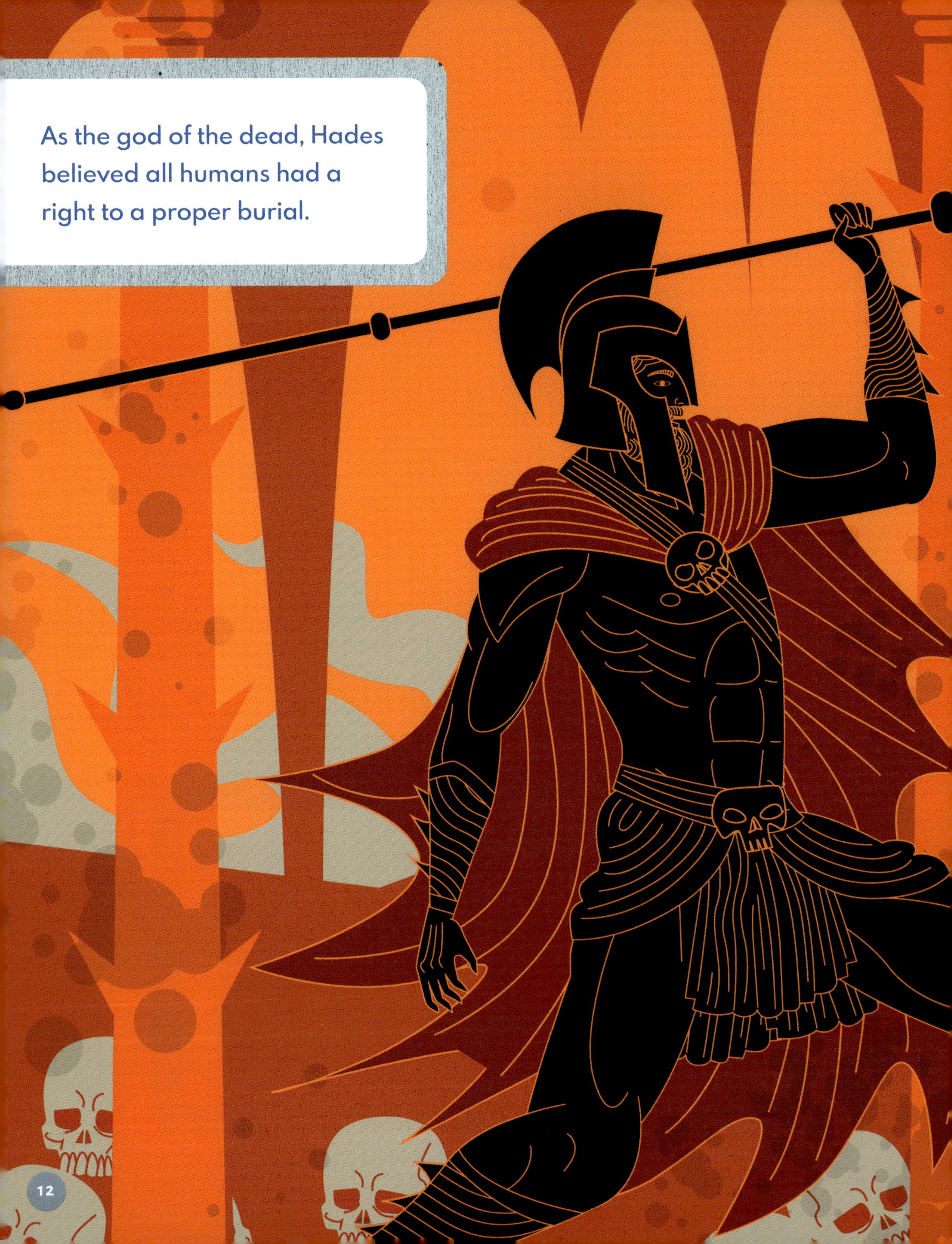

As the god of the dead, Hades believed all humans had a right to a proper burial.

RULER OF THE DEAD

Hades's parents were Cronus and Rhea. They were two of the mighty gods known as Titans. The Titans ruled over Earth. Cronus was their leader. Hades also had powerful siblings, such as Zeus and Poseidon. They fought to take control away from Cronus.

The Three Major Gods

Zeus was the god of the sky and weather.

Poseidon was the god of earthquakes, horses, and the sea.

Hades was the god of the underworld.

Zeus, Poseidon, and Hades were three important gods in Greek mythology. They each had special roles to play.

After a ten-year war, they defeated their father. Then they had to decide who would rule over the different parts of Earth. Hades got the underworld. It was a dark, gloomy place.

Hades rarely left the underworld. He tried to stay away from the other gods and the living. Hades was instead surrounded by the dead. All human souls eventually ended up in the underworld.

Guarding the Dead

Hades did not decide who lived and who died. Instead, he watched over the souls of the dead. Hades made sure they never left the underworld. He was fierce, grim, and stern, but he was not evil.

The god Hermes guided souls to the underworld. A boatman named Charon then sailed the souls across a river. This river kept the living away from the dead.

It cost the dead a coin to make the boat ride. Before they were buried, their families put one coin in their mouths. If the ancient Greeks didn't do this, they thought their loved ones would stay on Earth as ghosts.

The God of Death

Although Hades was the god of the dead, he was not the god of death. That title belonged to Thanatos. Thanatos represented nonviolent death. His sisters, the Keres, were spirits of cruel or violent death.

Charon is sometimes shown in artwork as a gloomy older man.

Cerberus was a monstrous, fierce watchdog.

A three-headed dog named Cerberus guarded the gates of the underworld. Cerberus made sure the souls did not escape. The dog also made sure the living did not get inside.

When they arrived, the souls were judged for the decisions they made while alive. Bad souls would get punished. Hades **supervised** trials and punishments. But he did not judge or punish souls himself.

PRIMARY SOURCE

A group of authors wrote about grief and death in Greek culture:

> In the Greek mythology, the dead journeyed to the Afterlife, ruled by Hades. Death was not [seen] as an end in and by itself, but rather as another "world" to belong to.

Source: Kyriaki Mystakidou et al. "Death and Grief in the Greek Culture," *SAGE Journals*, 1 Feb. 2005, journals.sagepub.com. Accessed 9 June 2021.

What's the Big Idea?

Read this quote carefully. What is its main idea? Explain how the main idea is supported by details.

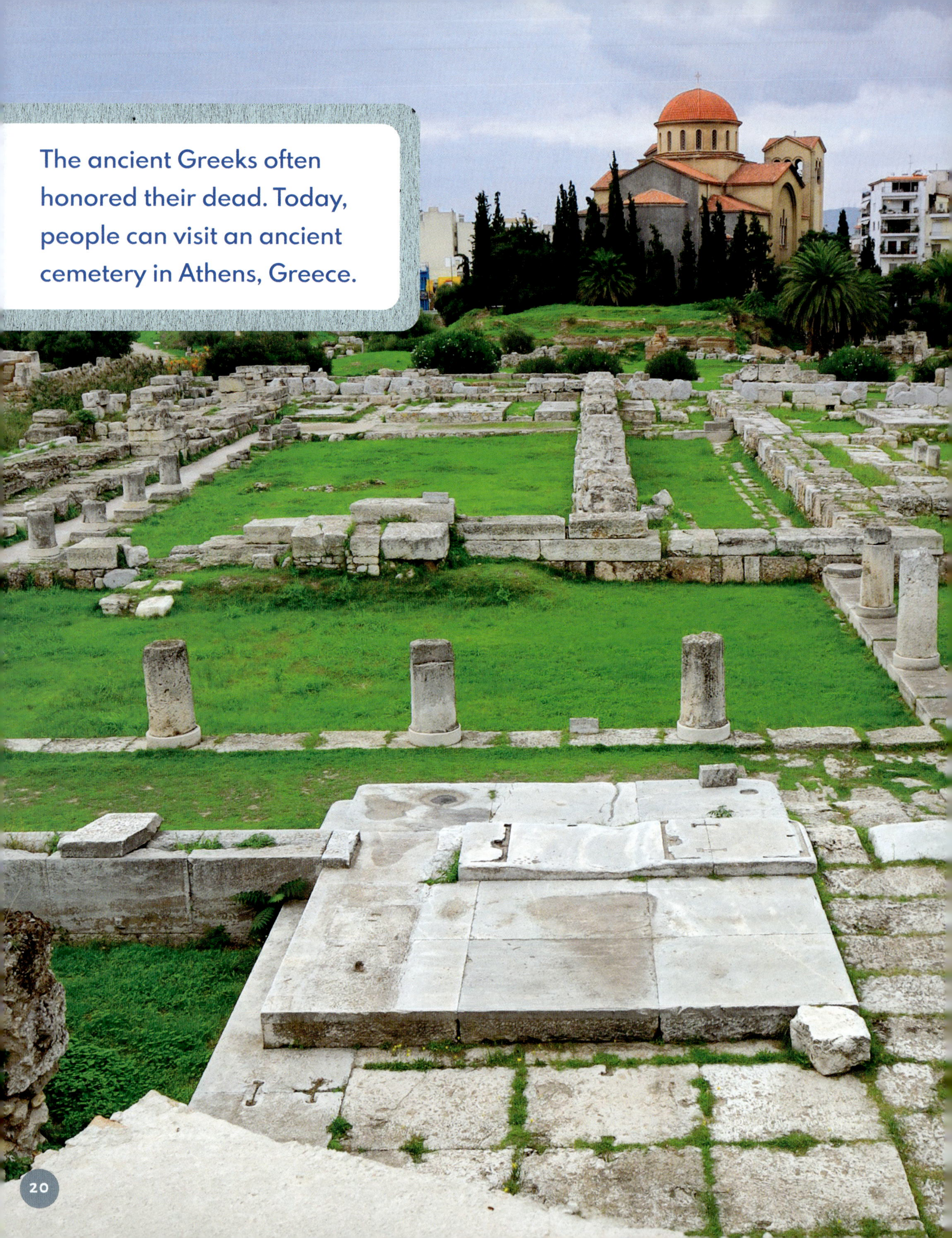

The ancient Greeks often honored their dead. Today, people can visit an ancient cemetery in Athens, Greece.

UNHAPPY HADES

Hades did not wish anyone harm. But he did represent death. Ancient Greeks were terrified of Hades. They refused to say his name. Instead, they called him the Renowned, Good Counsellor, the Host of Many, the Unseen One, and the Other Zeus.

Hades is sometimes seen as a scary figure.

Very few people worshipped Hades. **Temples** were rarely built in his honor. One temple for him was built in Elis. It would open once a year. Only a single priest was allowed to enter.

Rarely Seen or Heard

Ancient Greeks did not like to think about death. So they did not talk about Hades. They didn't want the god to notice them. They thought he might pull them into the underworld. There are very few myths and artworks about Hades for these reasons.

The Wealth Giver

Hades is known as the giver of wealth. That's because important metals, gems, and other riches are found underground. In addition, people believed he helped make Earth's soil healthy so plants could grow.

Artists have many different ideas of how the underworld looks.

One famous statue shows Hades carrying Persephone away.

When he was shown in art, Hades often looked like an older man with a beard. He would sometimes wear a crown. The crown sometimes had sunrays coming out of it.

People today still enjoy learning about the god of the underworld.

Hades would have an angry, serious, or sad look on his face.

Hades would often carry a **scepter** as a sign of his power. Sometimes he held keys to the underworld. This represented how souls could not leave once inside. Cerberus was often shown next to Hades. Even though the ancient Greeks didn't talk about Hades very much, he was still an important figure. Myths about him live on today.

Explore Online

Visit the website below. Does it give any new information about Hades or the underworld?

Underworld Gods

abdocorelibrary.com/hades

LEGENDARY FACTS

Hades was the god of the underworld. He was a powerful god. His brothers were Zeus and Poseidon.

The ancient Greeks were scared to speak Hades's name. They didn't build many temples for him. They also didn't put him on a lot of art.

The three-headed dog Cerberus helped Hades watch over the underworld.

Hades took Persephone away from her mother. Demeter was so upset that she caused winter.

Glossary

chariot
a small carriage with two wheels

civilization
a society that's organized and developed

scepter
a staff or rod carried by a ruler to show authority

souls
people's spirits, which include their thoughts and feelings

supervised
to have watched over and guided others

temple
a building used for worship

Online Resources

To learn more about Hades, visit our free resource websites below.

Visit **abdocorelibrary.com** or scan this QR code for free Common Core resources for teachers and students, including vetted activities, multimedia, and booklinks, for deeper subject comprehension.

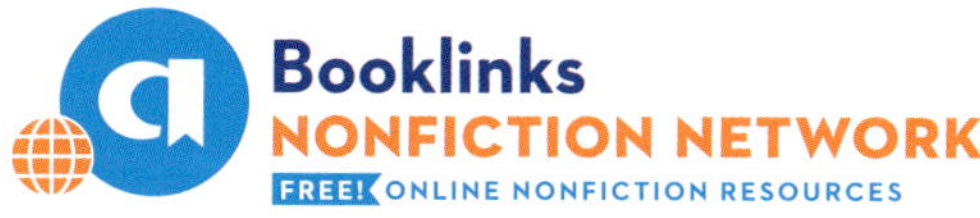

Visit **abdobooklinks.com** or scan this QR code for free additional online weblinks for further learning. These links are routinely monitored and updated to provide the most current information available.

Learn More

Hudak, Heather C. *Zeus.* Abdo, 2022.

Menzies, Jean. *Greek Myths.* DK, 2020.

Index

About the Author

Heather C. Hudak has written hundreds of books on all kinds of topics. She loves to travel when she's not writing. Hudak has visited about 60 countries. She has seen many ancient sites dedicated to the gods and goddesses of Greek mythology.